TRACING ROOTS

A STEP-BY-STEP GUIDE TO DISCOVERING YOUR ANCESTRY

Penelope Green

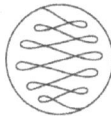

GLOBAL
PUBLISHING
SOLUTIONS

TRACING ROOTS: A STEP-BY-STEP GUIDE TO DISCOVERING OUR ANCESTRY by Penelope Green

Published by Global Publishing Solutions, LLC
923 Fieldside Drive
Matteson, Illinois 60443
www.globalpublishingsolutions.com

Library of Congress Control Number:
2023941355
International Standard Book Number:
979-8-9886045-0-1
E-book International Standard Book Number:
979-8-9886045-1-8

Printed in the United States of America

TABLE OF CONTENTS

THE IMPORTANCE OF GENEALOGY RESEARCH

Introduction

Genealogy is the study of family history and lineage. It involves tracing one's ancestry through historical records, interviews with family members, and DNA testing. Genealogy research has become increasingly popular in recent years, with the rise of online genealogy databases and DNA testing kits. In this chapter, we will explore the importance of genealogy research and the benefits it can provide.

Benefits of Genealogy Research

1. Understanding Your Family History

Genealogy research allows you to learn about your family's history, traditions, and culture. It helps you understand where you came from and how your ancestors lived. By discovering your family history, you can gain a deeper appreciation for your roots and the struggles and triumphs that your ancestors experienced.

2. Connecting with Your Family

Genealogy research provides an opportunity to connect with family members, both past and present. It can help you uncover stories about your ancestors that have been passed down through the generations. It can also lead to new connections with living relatives that you may not have known existed. By sharing your research with family members, you can strengthen your family ties and build a sense of community.

3. Preserving Your Family Legacy

Genealogy research allows you to document and preserve your family's history for future generations. By compiling information about your ancestors, you can create a record of your family's legacy that can be passed down through the generations. This is especially important for families who have experienced displacement, migration, or other events that have disrupted their family history.

4. Exploring Your Identity

Genealogy research can help you explore your identity and understand your place in the world. By discovering your family history, you can gain insights into your cultural heritage, traditions, and values. This can provide a sense of belonging and connection to your ancestors and the larger community from which you come.

How Discovering Your Ancestry Can Shape Your Identity and Provide a Sense of Belonging

1. Cultural Heritage

Genealogy research can help you understand your cultural heritage and the traditions that have been passed down through your family. This can provide a sense of connection to your ancestors and the larger community from which you come. It can also help you understand your place in the world and how your family's traditions and beliefs have shaped your identity.

2. Family Stories

Genealogy research can uncover family stories and traditions that have been passed down through the generations. These stories can provide insight into your family's values, struggles, and triumphs. They can also help you connect with your family and gain a deeper understanding of your family history.

3. Identity and Belonging

Genealogy research can provide a sense of identity and belonging. By discovering your family history, you can gain a sense of connection to your ancestors and the larger community from which you come. This can provide a sense of purpose and belonging that is essential to our well-being.

4. Sense of Continuity

Genealogy research can help us understand our place in history and provide a sense of continuity. By learning about our family's history, we can understand how our ancestors have contributed to the world and how we are connected to that legacy. This can provide a sense of continuity and purpose that is essential to our well-being.

Conclusion

Genealogy research is an important tool for understanding our family history and our place in the world. By uncovering our family's history, we can gain a deeper appreciation for our roots and the struggles and triumphs of our ancestors. We can also connect with living relatives and strengthen our family ties. Ultimately, genealogy research can provide a sense of identity and belonging that is essential to our well-being.

GATHERING INFORMATION FROM FAMILY MEMBERS

Introduction

Family members are a valuable source of information when it comes to genealogy research. They can provide insight into family traditions, stories, and important details that can help uncover your family history. However, approaching relatives for information can sometimes be a sensitive topic, especially if family members have different perspectives or experiences. In this chapter, we will explore tips for approaching relatives for information, questions to ask to uncover important family stories and details, and the importance of verifying information with primary sources.

Tips on How to Approach Relatives for Information

1. Start with a Plan

Before approaching relatives for information, it's important to have a plan in place. Determine which family members you want to speak with and what information you hope to gather from each. Consider scheduling a time to meet or setting up a phone call to discuss family history.

2. Be Respectful

When approaching relatives for information, it's important to be respectful of their time and their memories. Start by explaining why you are interested in family history and why it's important to you. Be mindful that some family members may be hesitant to discuss certain topics or may have different perspectives on family history.

3. Ask Open-Ended Questions

When gathering information from family members, it's important to ask open-ended questions that encourage them to share their memories and stories. Avoid asking yes or no questions or questions that can be answered with a single word. Instead, ask questions that encourage conversation and provide an opportunity for family members to share their experiences.

4. Take Notes

During conversations with family members, be sure to take detailed notes. Record important dates, names, and events, as well as any stories or memories that are shared. Be sure to ask permission before recording conversations, as some family members may prefer to speak off the record.

5. Follow Up

After gathering information from family members, be sure to follow up with any additional questions or requests for clarification. This can help ensure that you have a complete understanding of your family history and can help fill in any gaps in your research.

Questions to Ask to Uncover Important Family Stories and Details

1. Family History

Ask family members about their parents, grandparents, and other ancestors. Gather information about where they were born, where they lived, and any significant events or accomplishments in their lives.

2. Family Traditions

Ask family members about family traditions and customs. This can include religious or cultural practices, holiday celebrations, and family recipes.

3. Family Stories

Ask family members to share stories about their experiences growing up, family members who have passed away, and other significant events in the family's history. This can provide important details about your family's past and help you gain a deeper understanding of your family's identity.

4. Photos and Documents

Ask family members if they have any photos or documents that can help provide insight into your family history. This can include old family photos, birth certificates, marriage licenses, and other important documents.

The Importance of Verifying Information with Primary Sources

1. Accuracy

Verifying information with primary sources is essential to ensuring the accuracy of your family history research. Primary sources provide firsthand accounts of events and can help confirm information that has been passed down through generations.

2. Avoiding Errors

Without verifying information with primary sources, there is a risk of errors or inaccuracies in your family history research. Information that has been passed down through generations can sometimes be altered or misrepresented, so it's important to confirm details with primary sources.

3. Validation

Verifying information with primary sources can provide validation for your research and help build a more complete picture of your family history. It can also help you uncover new information and lead to new avenues of research.

Conclusion

Gathering information from family members is an important step in genealogy.

UTILIZING CENSUS AND VITAL RECORDS

Introduction

Census and vital records are essential resources for genealogists. They provide valuable information about our ancestors, including names, dates of birth, marriage, and death, and locations. Census records can help trace our family back through generations, while vital records can confirm relationships and help fill in missing gaps in our family tree. In this chapter, we will explore how to use census records to trace your family back through generations, the significance of vital records in genealogy research, and how to locate and access these records.

How to Use Census Records to Trace Your Family Back Through Generations

Census records are a valuable source of information for genealogists. The United States government has conducted a census every ten years since 1790. Each census provides information about individuals living in the United States, including their names, ages, occupations, and places of birth. Here are some tips on how to use census records to trace your family back through generations:

1. Start with the most recent census.

The most recent census available to the public is the 1940 census. Start by searching for your ancestors in the most recent census and work backward. As you move further back in time, the information available in the census records becomes less detailed.

2. Look for the head of the household.

In census records, the head of the household is usually listed first. Look for your ancestors by searching for their name or by searching for the head of the household's name. Once you have located the head of the household, you can look for other family members living in the same household.

3. Pay attention to details.

Census records can provide a wealth of information about your ancestors. Pay attention to details such as age, occupation, and place of birth. This information can help you confirm relationships and fill in missing gaps in your family tree.

4. Verify information with other sources.

While census records can provide valuable information, it's important to verify information with other sources. Census records can sometimes contain errors or inconsistencies, so it's important to confirm details with other records, such as vital records or military records.

Vital Records and Their Significance in Genealogy Research

Vital records are documents that record important life events, such as births, marriages, and deaths. These records are essential for genealogy research, as they provide valuable information about our ancestors, including names, dates of birth, marriage, and death, and locations. Here are some of the most common types of vital records and their significance in genealogy research:

1. Birth Certificates

Birth certificates are documents that record the birth of an individual. They provide information about the individual's name, date of birth, place of birth, and parents' names. Birth certificates can help confirm relationships and provide important information about our ancestors' early lives.

2. Marriage Certificates

Marriage certificates are documents that record the marriage of two individuals. They provide information about the couple's names, dates of birth, place of birth, and parents' names. Marriage certificates can help confirm relationships and provide important information about our ancestors' families.

3. Death Certificates

Death certificates are documents that record the death of an individual. They provide information about the individual's name, date of death, place of death, cause of death, and parents' names. Death certificates can help confirm relationships and provide important information about our ancestors' lives.

How to Locate and Access Census and Vital Records

Locating and accessing census and vital records can be a challenge, but there are several resources available to help genealogists. Here are some tips on how to locate and access census and vital records:

1. National Archives and Records Administration (NARA)

The National Archives and Records Administration (NARA) is the official repository for federal records, including census and military records. Many census records are available on their website, and they also offer research services for a fee. Vital records are typically held at the state or county level, so NARA may not be the best resource for accessing those records.

2. State Vital Records Offices

Each state has a vital records office that holds birth, marriage, and death certificates. Some states may have restrictions on who can access these records and what information is available. Check with the state vital records office for more information.

3. County Courthouses

County courthouses are often the best resource for accessing vital records. Many courthouses hold birth, marriage, and death records dating back to the 1800s or earlier. Contact the county courthouse where your ancestors lived to see what records are available and how to access them.

4. Online Databases

There are many online databases available for genealogy research, including Ancestry.com, FamilySearch.org, and MyHeritage.com. These databases offer access to census and vital records, as well as other genealogy resources. Some require a subscription or a fee for access, while others are free.

Conclusion

Census and vital records are essential resources for genealogists. They provide valuable information about our ancestors and help us trace our family back through generations. Using census records, we can uncover details about our ancestors' lives, such as their occupation, place of birth, and family members. Vital records, such as birth, marriage, and death certificates, can confirm relationships and provide important information about our ancestors' lives. By utilizing these resources and verifying information with other sources, we can piece together our family history and gain a better understanding of our identity and sense of belonging.

EXPLORING HISTORICAL RECORDS AND ARCHIVES

Introduction

Historical records and archives can provide a wealth of information for genealogists. These records can help us understand our ancestors' lives and provide insights into the communities and societies they lived in. In this chapter, we will explore some of the historical records and archives that are available to genealogists, including wills, probate records, and military records. We will also discuss how to access and interpret these records.

Wills

Wills are legal documents that outline how a person's assets will be distributed after their death. Wills can provide valuable information for genealogists, including the names of family members and details about the person's property and assets. Wills can also provide clues about family relationships, such as if a person left their property to a spouse or children.

Wills are typically held at the county courthouse or state archives, depending on the state. Some states may have restrictions on who can access wills and what information is available. Check with the local courthouse or state archives for more information on accessing wills.

Probate Records

Probate records are court records that document the distribution of a person's assets after their death. Probate records can provide valuable information for genealogists, including the names of family members and details about the person's property and assets.

Probate records can also provide information about family relationships, such as if a person left their property to a spouse or children. Probate records may also include wills, inventories of assets, and other legal documents.

Probate records are typically held at the county courthouse or state archives, depending on the state. Some states may have restrictions on who can access probate records and what information is available. Check with the local courthouse or state archives for more information on accessing probate records.

Military Records

Military records can provide valuable information for genealogists, including details about a person's military service and their involvement in historical events. Military records can also provide information about a person's family, such as their next of kin or spouse.

Military records are typically held at the National Archives and Records Administration (NARA). NARA holds military records from all branches of the military, dating back to the Revolutionary War. To access military records, you will need to submit a request to NARA.

Interpreting Historical Records

Interpreting historical records can be challenging, as the language and writing style may be different from modern-day English. Additionally, some records may be difficult to read due to age or damage.

To interpret historical records, it is important to have a basic understanding of the time period and context in which the records were created. You may also need to consult historical dictionaries or other resources to decipher unfamiliar words or phrases.

Conclusion

Historical records and archives can provide a wealth of information for genealogists. Wills, probate records, and military records can help us understand our ancestors' lives and provide insights into the communities and societies they lived in. By accessing and interpreting these records, we can piece together our family history and gain a better understanding of our identity and sense of belonging.

USING DNA TESTING TO ENHANCE RESEARCH

Introduction

DNA testing has revolutionized genealogy research, providing a powerful tool for identifying relatives and tracing family history. In this chapter, we will explore the basics of DNA testing and how it can be used in genealogy research. We will also discuss the different types of DNA tests available and their benefits, as well as how to interpret DNA test results and incorporate them into your research.

The Basics of DNA Testing

DNA testing is a method of analyzing a person's genetic code to identify inherited traits and potential genetic disorders. In genealogy research, DNA testing can be used to identify relatives and confirm family relationships.

DNA is made up of a sequence of nucleotides, which are the building blocks of DNA. The sequence of nucleotides determines an individual's genetic code. There are different types of DNA that can be analyzed in genealogy research, including autosomal DNA, mitochondrial DNA (mtDNA), and Y-chromosome DNA (Y-DNA).

Autosomal DNA is inherited from both parents and can provide information about relatives on both sides of the family. Mitochondrial DNA is inherited from the mother and can be used to trace maternal ancestry. Y-chromosome DNA is inherited from the father and can be used to trace paternal ancestry.

Types of DNA Tests Available

There are different types of DNA tests available for genealogy research, each with its own benefits. These include:

1. Autosomal DNA Testing: This test analyzes autosomal DNA and can identify relatives on both sides of the family. Autosomal DNA testing is the most commonly used DNA test in genealogy research.

2. Mitochondrial DNA Testing: This test analyzes mtDNA and can be used to trace maternal ancestry. Mitochondrial DNA testing is useful for tracing ancestry back many generations.

3. Y-Chromosome DNA Testing: This test analyzes Y-DNA and can be used to trace paternal ancestry. Y-chromosome DNA testing is useful for tracing ancestry back many generations.

Interpreting DNA Test Results

Interpreting DNA test results can be challenging, as the results may be complex and difficult to understand. It is important to have a basic understanding of DNA testing and the different types of DNA that can be analyzed.

Autosomal DNA test results will provide a list of potential relatives, ranked by the amount of DNA they share with you. The amount of DNA shared can provide clues about the nature of the relationship, such as whether the person is a close relative or a more distant cousin.

Mitochondrial DNA test results will provide information about the maternal lineage. Mitochondrial DNA testing is most useful for tracing ancestry back many generations.

Y-chromosome DNA test results will provide information about the paternal lineage. Y-chromosome DNA testing is most useful for tracing ancestry back many generations.

Incorporating DNA Test Results into Your Research

DNA test results can be incorporated into your genealogy research to help confirm family relationships and identify potential relatives. DNA test results can also provide clues about ancestry that may not be evident in traditional genealogy research.

When incorporating DNA test results into your research, it is important to verify the results using traditional genealogy research methods. DNA test results should be used as a supplement to traditional research, not as a replacement for it.

Conclusion

DNA testing can be a powerful tool for genealogy research, providing insights into family relationships and ancestry that may not be evident in traditional research methods. By understanding the basics of DNA testing, the different types of DNA tests available, and how to interpret DNA test results, you can enhance your genealogy research and gain a better understanding of your family history.

OVERCOMING CHALLENGES AND BRICK WALLS

Introduction

Genealogy research can be a fascinating and rewarding pursuit, but it is not without its challenges. At times, genealogists may encounter roadblocks or brick walls that seem impossible to overcome. In this chapter, we will explore some of the common challenges encountered in genealogy research and provide tips for overcoming them.

Common Challenges in Genealogy Research

1. Lack of Information: One of the most common challenges in genealogy research is a lack of information. This can be due to a variety of factors, such as lost records, incomplete family trees, or relatives who do not wish to share information.

2. Misinformation: Another challenge in genealogy research is misinformation. This can include inaccurate information passed down through family stories, as well as errors in official records.

3. Language Barriers: Genealogy research often requires accessing records and resources in different languages. Language barriers can make it difficult to interpret records and communicate with relatives in other countries.

4. Limited Access to Records: Access to records can also be a challenge in genealogy research. Some records may be restricted due to privacy laws, while others may be difficult to access due to their location or condition.

Tips for Overcoming Brick Walls

1. Review Your Research: When you hit a brick wall in your genealogy research, the first step is to review your research. Check for errors or inconsistencies in your family tree and ensure that you have gathered all available information.
2. Expand Your Search: If you have exhausted all available resources in your current search, it may be time to expand your search. This can involve looking for alternative records or searching in different locations.
3. Collaborate with Other Genealogists: Collaborating with other genealogists can be a valuable resource in overcoming brick walls. Other genealogists may have access to different resources or have expertise in areas where you are struggling.
4. Utilize DNA Testing: DNA testing can be a powerful tool in overcoming brick walls in genealogy research. DNA testing can provide clues about potential relatives and confirm family relationships.

5. Seek Professional Help: If you have tried all other options and are still unable to break through a brick wall, seeking professional help may be the best option. Professional genealogists have expertise in accessing records and resources that may not be available to the general public.

Conclusion

Genealogy research can be a challenging but rewarding pursuit. When faced with challenges or brick walls in your research, it is important to take a step back and review your research. Consider expanding your search, collaborating with other genealogists, utilizing DNA testing, and seeking professional help if necessary. With persistence and dedication, you can overcome challenges and make exciting discoveries in your family history.

PRESERVING AND SHARING YOUR FINDINGS

Introduction

After investing countless hours and effort into genealogy research, it is important to document and preserve your findings for future generations. In this chapter, we will explore some of the best practices for preserving and sharing your research. From creating a comprehensive family tree to sharing your findings with others, we will provide tips for ensuring that your research is accessible and meaningful for years to come.

Documenting Your Research

1. Create a Comprehensive Family Tree: One of the best ways to document your research is by creating a comprehensive family tree. This can be done using online genealogy software or through a physical family tree chart. Be sure to include as much information as possible, such as birth dates, marriage dates, and locations.

2. Organize Your Documents: Genealogy research involves a lot of paperwork, from census records to vital records. To ensure that your research is easily accessible and organized, consider

creating a filing system. Use folders or binders to separate documents by surname or family member.

3. Use Online Tools: There are many online tools available for documenting and organizing your genealogy research. Websites such as Ancestry and FamilySearch allow you to store and share your research with others.

Preserving Your Research

1. Store Documents Properly: To ensure that your documents last for years to come, it is important to store them properly. Use acid-free paper and folders and avoid exposing documents to sunlight or moisture.

2. Digitize Your Documents: Another way to preserve your research is by digitizing your documents. This can be done using a scanner or camera. Be sure to save digital copies in multiple locations, such as on an external hard drive or cloud storage.

3. Back Up Your Data: In addition to digitizing your documents, it is important to back up your data regularly. Consider using an online backup service or external hard drive to ensure that your research is not lost in the event of a computer failure.

Sharing Your Findings

1. Host Family Reunions: Hosting family reunions is a great way to share your research with others. Consider creating a family tree display or sharing interesting stories about your ancestors.
2. Create a Family Newsletter: A family newsletter is a fun and creative way to share your genealogy research with others. Include updates on your research, stories about ancestors, and photos.
3. Use Social Media: Social media platforms such as Facebook and Instagram can also be used to share your research with others. Create a family group or page and share interesting stories and photos.

Conclusion

Preserving and sharing your genealogy research is important not only for your own personal satisfaction but also for future generations. Documenting your research, preserving your documents, and sharing your findings with others are all key components of ensuring that your research is accessible and meaningful for years to come. Consider using a combination of online tools, physical documentation, and creative sharing methods to ensure that your research is both comprehensive and accessible.

CASE STUDIES

In this chapter, we will explore real-life case studies that demonstrate the power of genealogy research to uncover fascinating family stories and connect people with their past. These examples will illustrate the methods and techniques outlined in the previous chapters, including gathering information from family members, utilizing census and vital records, exploring historical records and archives, using DNA testing, and overcoming challenges and brick walls. These case studies will also demonstrate the importance of preserving and sharing your findings.

Case Study 1: Tracing a Family Lineage through Census Records Ms. Johnson wanted to trace her family lineage back to the early 1800s, but she hit a brick wall when she couldn't find any records beyond her great-grandparents. She decided to use census records to continue her search. Using her great-grandparents' names and approximate birth dates, she was able to locate them in the 1900 and 1910 census records. Through this information, she was able to determine their parents' names and continue tracing her lineage back to the early 1800s. This case study shows that census records can be a valuable tool for tracing family lineages and that utilizing information from multiple census records can provide a more complete picture of your family history.

Case Study 2: Uncovering a Family Secret through DNA Testing

Mr. Garcia was interested in learning more about his family history, but he was adopted and didn't have any information about his biological family. He decided to take a DNA test to learn more about his ancestry. The test results revealed a close genetic match with a woman named Maria, who turned out to be his biological half-sister. Through further research, Mr. Garcia learned that his biological mother had given him up for adoption as a young child. While this information was difficult to process, it provided Mr. Garcia with a better understanding of his family history. This case study demonstrates that DNA testing can uncover family secrets and provide insight into biological connections, and that it is important to approach sensitive information with care and sensitivity.

Case Study 3: Using Historical Records to Trace Military Service

Mr. Smith wanted to learn more about his grandfather's military service during World War II. He knew that his grandfather had served in the Army, but he didn't have any other information. He decided to search for military records through the National Archives. He was able to locate his grandfather's service records, which included information about his assignments, promotions, and awards. He also found a photograph of his grandfather in uniform, which was a valuable addition to his family's collection of memorabilia. This case study demonstrates that historical records such as military records can provide valuable information about family members' service and accomplishments, and that the National Archives and other government agencies can be valuable resources for finding historical records.

Case Study 4: Overcoming a Brick Wall through Collaboration Ms. Brown had been researching her family history for several years but had hit a brick wall when she couldn't find any information about her great-great-grandmother's parents. She decided to reach out to other genealogy researchers to see if they had any information. Through a genealogy forum, she connected with another researcher who had been looking for information about the same family. Together, they were able to piece together information from various sources, including census records and marriage licenses, to trace the family lineage back several generations. This case study shows that collaboration with other genealogy researchers can be a valuable tool for overcoming brick walls, and that genealogy forums and online communities can provide opportunities for connecting with other researchers.

These case studies demonstrate the power of genealogy research to uncover fascinating family stories and connect people with their past in new and unexpected ways. By following the methods outlined in the previous chapters, you too can explore your own family history and discover the stories of your ancestors.

TAKING YOUR RESEARCH TO THE NEXT LEVEL

Genealogy research can be a challenging and rewarding pursuit. Whether you are just starting out or have been researching your family history for years, there is always more to learn and explore. In this chapter, we will discuss resources and tips for advanced genealogy research, as well as how to network with other genealogy researchers and professionals.

Resources for Advanced Genealogy Research

There are many resources available to genealogy researchers that can help take their research to the next level. Here are a few to consider:

1. DNA Testing: DNA testing has become increasingly popular in recent years and can provide valuable information for genealogy researchers. DNA testing can help confirm relationships, identify genetic health risks, and connect individuals with potential relatives. There are several companies that offer DNA testing services, including AncestryDNA, 23andMe, and MyHeritage.

2. Historical Newspapers: Historical newspapers can provide valuable information for genealogy researchers, such as birth,

marriage, and death announcements, obituaries, and news articles about specific events or individuals. Many historical newspapers have been digitized and can be accessed online through subscription services such as Newspapers.com or GenealogyBank.

3. Military Records: Military records can be a valuable resource for genealogy researchers, providing information about an individual's military service, such as enlistment dates, rank, and unit information. These records can often be accessed through the National Archives and Records Administration (NARA) or through online genealogy databases such as Ancestry.com.

4. Land Records: Land records can provide valuable information about an individual's land ownership and property transactions. These records can often be accessed through county or state archives, or through online genealogy databases.

5. Probate Records: Probate records can provide valuable information about an individual's estate, including wills, inventories, and property appraisals. These records can often be accessed through county or state archives, or through online genealogy databases.

Tips for Advanced Genealogy Research

In addition to utilizing the resources mentioned above, there are several tips and strategies that can help genealogy researchers take their research to the next level. Here are a few to consider:

1. Create a Research Plan: Before diving into a new research project, it's important to create a research plan that outlines your research objectives and the sources you plan to use. This can help ensure that you stay focused and organized throughout the research process.

2. Use Multiple Sources: When conducting genealogy research, it's important to use multiple sources to corroborate the information you find. This can help ensure that the information you uncover is accurate and reliable.

3. Take Detailed Notes: When conducting genealogy research, it's important to take detailed notes about the sources you use and the information you uncover. This can help you keep track of your research and avoid repeating work you've already done.

4. Join Genealogy Societies: Joining genealogy societies can provide valuable networking opportunities, as well as access to resources such as newsletters, journals, and educational events.

5. Attend Conferences: Genealogy conferences can provide valuable opportunities to learn from experts in the field, network with other researchers, and discover new resources and strategies for genealogy research.

Networking with Other Genealogy Researchers and Professionals

Networking with other genealogy researchers and professionals can be a valuable resource for genealogy researchers looking to take their research to the next level. Here are a few strategies for networking with other genealogy researchers and professionals:

1. Join Genealogy Societies: Joining genealogy societies can provide valuable networking opportunities, as well as access to resources such as newsletters, journals, and educational events.
2. Attend Conferences: Genealogy conferences can provide valuable opportunities to learn from experts in the field.

Join Genealogical Societies and Organizations

Joining genealogical societies and organizations is another way to network with other researchers and professionals and access resources for advanced genealogy research. These societies and organizations can provide you with access to specialized databases, archives, and libraries that may not be available elsewhere. You can also attend conferences, workshops, and seminars hosted by these societies to learn from experts in the field and connect with other genealogists.

There are many genealogical societies and organizations at the national, state, and local levels. Some of the most prominent national organizations include the National Genealogical Society, the Federation of Genealogical Societies, and the Association of Professional Genealogists. State-level organizations include the New England Historic Genealogical Society and the Ohio Genealogical Society, among many others. There are also many local genealogical societies that are often affiliated with larger organizations.

To find a genealogical society or organization that suits your needs, you can use online resources such as the Cyndi's List genealogy directory or the Directory of Genealogical and Historical Societies in the United States and Canada. You can also check with your local library or historical society to see if they know of any genealogical organizations in your area.

Attend Genealogy Conferences and Workshops

Attending genealogy conferences and workshops is another way to take your research to the next level. These events provide opportunities to learn from experts in the field, network with other genealogists, and gain access to specialized resources and databases.

Some of the most prominent genealogy conferences include RootsTech, the National Genealogical Society Conference, and the Federation of Genealogical Societies Conference. These events typically feature lectures, workshops, and exhibits on a wide range of genealogy topics, as well as opportunities to connect with other genealogists.

In addition to national conferences, there are also many regional and local genealogy conferences and workshops. These events may be hosted by genealogical societies, libraries, or other organizations.

Collaborate with Other Researchers

Collaborating with other genealogy researchers can be a valuable way to expand your research and uncover new information about your ancestors. You can collaborate with other researchers in a variety of ways, including:

- Joining genealogy groups on social media: There are many genealogy groups on Facebook and other social media platforms where you can connect with other researchers and share information and resources.

Participating in online forums: Online forums such as Genealogy

Utilize Advanced Research Techniques

Advanced genealogy research techniques can help you uncover more information about your ancestors and their lives. Some of these techniques include:

- DNA testing: DNA testing can help you identify relatives and ancestors and confirm relationships. There are several types of DNA tests available, including autosomal DNA tests, Y-DNA tests, and mtDNA tests.
- Cluster genealogy: Cluster genealogy involves researching the entire community or neighborhood in which your ancestors lived, rather than just focusing on your direct ancestors. This can help you uncover new information about your ancestors and their lives.

- Genetic genealogy: Genetic genealogy involves using DNA testing in combination with traditional genealogical research to uncover new information about your family history. This technique can help you identify relatives and ancestors, confirm relationships, and uncover new information about your ancestors.

- Reverse genealogy: Reverse genealogy involves tracing the descendants of a particular ancestor, rather than tracing the ancestors themselves. This can help you identify living relatives who may have information about your ancestors and their lives.

- Record analysis: Analyzing historical records such as census records, wills, and land deeds can help you uncover new information about your ancestors and their lives. Advanced record analysis techniques include cluster analysis, timeline analysis, and correlation analysis.

CONCLUSION

In this book, we have explored the exciting world of genealogy research, from the basics of getting started to the advanced techniques for taking your research to the next level. We have discussed the importance of discovering your ancestry and the many benefits that come with it. We have also shared resources and tips for overcoming common challenges and making the most of your research.

In this final chapter, we will recap the key takeaways of this book and discuss the significance of discovering your ancestry. We will also offer some encouragement and advice for continuing your journey of genealogy research.

Key Takeaways

Throughout this book, we have covered a lot of ground. Here are some of the key takeaways:

1. Start with what you know: The first step in genealogy research is to gather information from your family and personal records. This will help you build a solid foundation for your research.

2. Use a variety of sources: Don't rely on a single source for your research. Use a variety of sources, including online databases, archives, and libraries.

3. Organize your research: Keep track of your research in a systematic way. This will help you avoid duplicating efforts and keep track of your progress.

4. Take advantage of technology: There are many tools and resources available to genealogy researchers, including online databases, DNA testing, and software programs.

5. Be persistent: Genealogy research can be challenging and time-consuming. Don't give up if you hit a roadblock. Keep looking for new sources of information and keep asking questions.

The Significance of Discovering Your Ancestry

Discovering your ancestry can be a life-changing experience. It can help you better understand your family history and your place in the world. Here are some of the ways that discovering your ancestry can be significant:

1. Connecting with the past: Learning about your ancestors can help you connect with the past and better understand the context in which they lived.

2. Understanding your heritage: Discovering your ancestry can help you better understand your heritage and the cultural and ethnic traditions that are part of your family history.

3. Building a sense of identity: Knowing your family history can help you build a sense of identity and a connection to your roots.

4. Connecting with family: Genealogy research can help you connect with relatives you may not have known existed and build stronger relationships with the family members you do know.

5. Honoring your ancestors: Discovering your ancestry can be a way to honor the legacy of your ancestors and the contributions they made to their communities and to your family.

Encouragement to Continue Your Journey

Genealogy research is a lifelong journey. There is always more to discover and new challenges to overcome. Here are some tips for continuing your journey:

1. Stay organized: As you continue your research, it is important to stay organized. Keep track of your research in a systematic way and stay on top of new information.

2. Keep learning: There is always more to learn about genealogy research. Take advantage of online resources, books, and other materials to continue your education.

3. Share your findings: Share your research with family members and other genealogy researchers. This can help you make new connections and discover new information.

4. Join a genealogy society: Joining a genealogy society can be a great way to connect with other researchers and get access to additional resources.

5. Don't give up: Genealogy research can be frustrating at times, but don't give up. Stay persistent and keep looking for new sources of information.

Conclusion

Genealogy research is a journey that can be both rewarding and life changing. Whether you're just starting out or have years of experience, there is always more to discover and new challenges to overcome. This book has provided you with tips and advice to help you uncover the stories of your ancestors and gain a deeper understanding of your personal history. Remember, genealogy research is a never-ending journey, but the rewards are immeasurable. As you continue on your journey, don't give up. Keep searching, keep learning, and keep exploring. The world of genealogy is vast, and there may always be something new to discover or learn. Keep networking with other genealogy researchers and professionals, and don't be afraid to reach out for help when you need it. In conclusion, genealogy research is a journey that connects us to our past and helps us understand our present. By following the tips and resources outlined in this guide, you can take your genealogy research to the next level and uncover even more about your family history. So, keep exploring, keep asking questions, and most importantly, keep connecting with your ancestors and the rich tapestry of your family's history. Happy researching!

.

www.ingramcontent.com/pod-product-compliance
Lightning Source LLC
Chambersburg PA
CBHW070031030426
42335CB00017B/2383